LET'S PLAY FLUTE!

COMPANION TO LET'S PLAY FLUTE! METHOD BOOK 2

by Elisabeth Weinzierl & Edmund Waechter

Repertoire Correlates to
Let's Play Flute! Method Book 2
50600097

To access companion recorded accompaniments online, visit:
www.halleonard.com/mylibrary

Enter Code
6396-7284-0683-5853

If you require a physical CD of the online audio that accompanies this book, please contact Hal Leonard Corporation at info@halleonard.com.

Sy. 2926

RICORDI

HAL•LEONARD®
CORPORATION
7777 W. BLUEMOUND RD. P.O. BOX 13819 MILWAUKEE, WI 53213

www.halleonard.com

Original publication: *Flöte Spielen Spielbuch B*, by Elisabeth Weinzierl and Edmund Waechter (Sy. 2942)
© 2014 by G. Ricordi & Co., Berlin
All rights reserved

English translation/adaptation: *Let's Play Flute! Repertoire Book 2*, by Elisabeth Weinzierl and Edmund Waechter
English translation/adaptation by Rachel Kelly
© 2015 by G. Ricordi & Co., Berlin
All rights reserved
Exclusively distributed by Hal Leonard MGB, a Hal Leonard Corporation company.

PREFACE

Let's Play Flute…

…and have fun making music with others! Learning the fundamentals of ensemble playing should accompany and enrich private instrumental instruction from the very beginning. In addition to being fun, the pedagogical importance of emphasizing chamber music techniques cannot be overstated. Rhythmic stability and intonation are naturally improved through ensemble playing, as are the ability to listen to others and react to them.

For this repertoire book, we have chosen eighteen songs, dances, character pieces, and classical melodies from various time periods and countries, that flute students are able to master quickly. The piano part has been arranged at a similar level of difficulty, so that two musicians of around the same age and/or level of experience may play together. Accompaniment recordings of the piano part give students the opportunity to practice with piano, even when a pianist is not available. For the faster pieces, both a slow tempo and a fast tempo accompaniment recording are provided.

—Elisabeth Weinzierl and Edmund Waechter

Some pieces have two accompaniment recordings. One is at a slower practice tempo, and the other is at a performance tempo. These are clearly indicated throughout.

TABLE OF CONTENTS

Repertoire correlates to *Method Book 2*

This table of contents is organized by the corresponding chapters in *Let's Play Flute! Method Book 2*. In addition, at the bottom of each page in this book, you will find a note that tells you from which chapter you will be able to play each piece. For example, if the bottom of the page states "*Let's Play Flute! Method Book 2,* Chapter 6," you will have learned all the notes for the piece once you have finished Chapter 6 in *Let's Play Flute! Method Book 2*.

Bourrée

from *Water Music*, HWV 349

Practice tempo: Andante
Performance tempo: Allegro

George Frideric Handel (1685–1759)
Arr.: E. Weinzierl / E. Waechter

Aura Lee

George R. Poulton (1828–1867)
Arr.: E. Weinzierl / E. Waechter

Elvis Presley used the melody from "Aura Lee" for his hit "Love Me Tender."

Grand Waltz

Francisco Tárrega (1852–1909)
Arr.: E. Weinzierl / E. Waechter

Allegro

Let's Play Flute! Method Book 2, Chapter 1   Sy. 2926   © 2015 by G. Ricordi & Co., Berlin

Viva Jujuy

Practice tempo: Adagio
Performance tempo: Allegro

Argentinian Song
Arr.: E. Weinzierl / E. Waechter

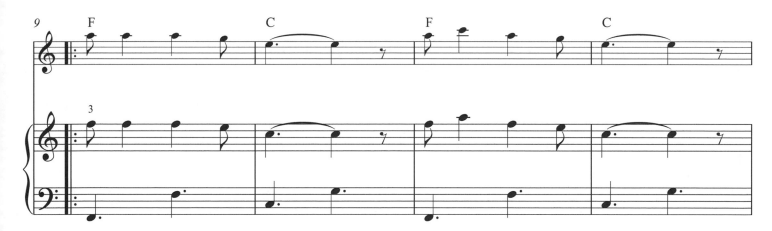

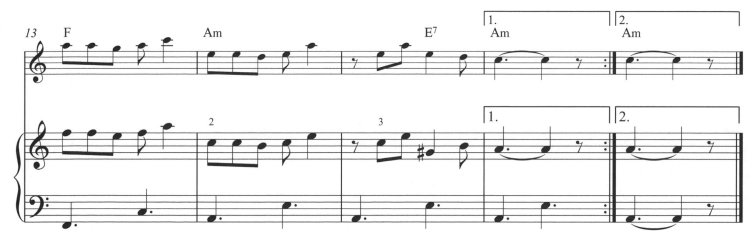

Sy. 2926

Lazy Luke

A Raggy Drag

George J. Philpot (dates unknown)
Arr.: E. Weinzierl / E. Waechter

Largo
(Ombra mai fù from the opera *Serse*)

George Frideric Handel (1685–1759)

Battare Prosciutto

Traditional Klezmer Tune
Arr.: E. Weinzierl / E. Waechter

Practice tempo: Andante
Performance tempo: Moderato

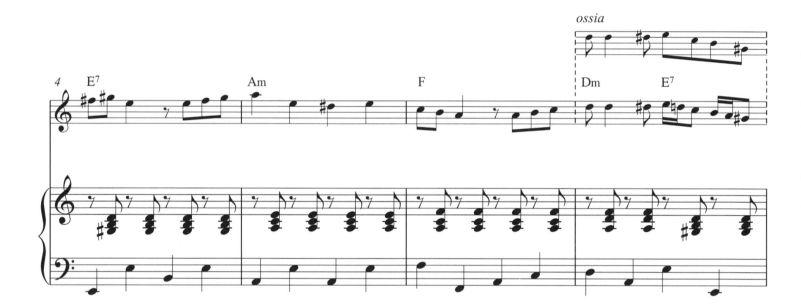

Sy. 2926

The Last Rose of Summer

Irish Melody
After: Friedrich Kuhlau (1786–1832) Op. 105

　　　　　　　Sy. 2926

LET'S PLAY FLUTE!

COMPANION TO LET'S PLAY FLUTE! METHOD BOOK 2

by Elisabeth Weinzierl & Edmund Waechter

Repertoire Correlates to
Let's Play Flute! Method Book 2
50600097

To access companion recorded accompaniments online, visit **www.halleonard.com/mylibrary**
and enter the access code printed on the title page of the piano score.

If you require a physical CD of the online audio that accompanies this book, please contact Hal Leonard Corporation at info@halleonard.com.

Sy. 2926

RICORDI

HAL•LEONARD®
CORPORATION

7777 W. BLUEMOUND RD. P.O. BOX 13819 MILWAUKEE, WI 53213

Original publication: *Flöte Spielen Spielbuch B*, by Elisabeth Weinzierl and Edmund Waechter (Sy. 2942)
© 2014 by G. Ricordi & Co., Berlin
All rights reserved

English translation/adaptation: *Let's Play Flute! Repertoire Book 2*, by Elisabeth Weinzierl and Edmund Waechter
English translation/adaptation by Rachel Kelly
© 2015 by G. Ricordi & Co., Berlin
All rights reserved
Exclusively distributed by Hal Leonard MGB, a Hal Leonard Corporation company.

www.halleonard.com

TABLE OF CONTENTS

This table of contents is organized by the corresponding chapters in *Let's Play Flute! Method Book 2*. In addition, at the bottom of each page in this book, you will find a note that tells you from which chapter you will be able to play each piece. For example, if the bottom of the page states "*Let's Play Flute! Method Book 2,* Chapter 6," you will have learned all the notes for the piece once you have finished Chapter 6 in *Let's Play Flute! Method Book 2*.

The price of this publication includes access to companion recorded accompaniments online, for download or streaming, using the unique code found on the title page of the piano score. Visit **www.halleonard.com/mylibrary** and enter the access code.

Some pieces have two accompaniment recordings. One is at a slower practice tempo, and the other is at a performance tempo. These are clearly indicated throughout.

Bourrée

from *Water Music*, HWV 349

Practice tempo: Andante
Performance tempo: Allegro

George Frideric Handel (1685–1759)
Arr.: E. Weinzierl / E. Waechter

Aura Lee

Andante

George R. Poulton (1828–1867)
Arr.: E. Weinzierl / E. Waechter

Elvis Presley used the melody from "Aura Lee" for his hit "Love Me Tender."

Sy. 2926

Grand Waltz

Francisco Tárrega (1852–1909)
Arr.: E. Weinzierl / E. Waechter

Viva Jujuy

Argentinian Song
Arr.: E. Weinzierl / E. Waechter

Practice tempo: Adagio
Performance tempo: Allegro

Let's Play Flute! Method Book 2, Chapter 1   Sy. 2926   © 2015 by G. Ricordi & Co., Berlin

Lazy Luke

A Raggy Drag

George J. Philpot (dates unknown)
Arr.: E. Weinzierl / E. Waechter

Sy. 2926

Largo
(Ombra mai fù from the opera *Serse*)

George Frideric Handel (1685–1759)

Let's Play Flute! Method Book 2, Chapter 2   Sy. 2926

Battare Prosciutto

Traditional Klezmer Tune
Arr.: E. Weinzierl / E. Waechter

Practice tempo: Andante
Performance tempo: Moderato

Sy. 2926

The Last Rose of Summer

Irish Melody
After: Friedrich Kuhlau (1786–1832) Op. 105

First Waltz

Traditional Klezmer Tune
Arr.: E. Weinzierl / E. Waechter

Fine

D. S. (%) al Fine

Andante
from Sonata Op. 99, No. 1

James Hook (1746–1827)

Albumblatt

from *Kolibris*, Op. 210

Emil Kronke (1865–1938)

Larghetto espressivo
from Sonata Op. 25, No. 1

Johann Ludwig Dussek (1760–1812)

Sy. 2926

Cantabile
from Sonata in G Major, TWV 41:G8

Georg Philipp Telemann (1681–1767)
Arr.: E. Weinzierl / E. Waechter

Largo

Let's Play Flute! Method Book 2, Chapter 6   Sy. 2926   © 2015 by G. Ricordi & Co., Berlin

Menuett
from Divertimento, KV 439b, No. 2

Wolfgang Amadeus Mozart (1756–1791)
Arr.: E. Weinzierl / E. Waechter

Sy. 2926

Barcarole

from the opera *Oberon*

Carl Maria von Weber (1786–1826)
Arr.: after Kaspar Kummer (1795–1870)

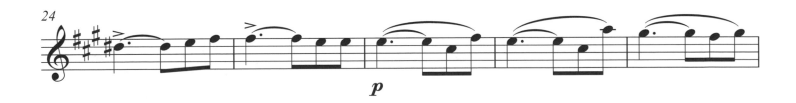

Let's Play Flute! Method Book 2, Chapter 6

Sy. 2926

Gavotte
from the opera *Rosine*

François-Joseph Gossec (1734–1829)
Arr.: E. Weinzierl / E. Waechter
(after Ary van Leeuwen)

D. C. al ⊕ - ⊕

Sy. 2926

This page has intentionally been left blank to facilitate page turns.

First Waltz

Traditional Klezmer Tune
Arr.: E. Weinzierl / E. Waechter

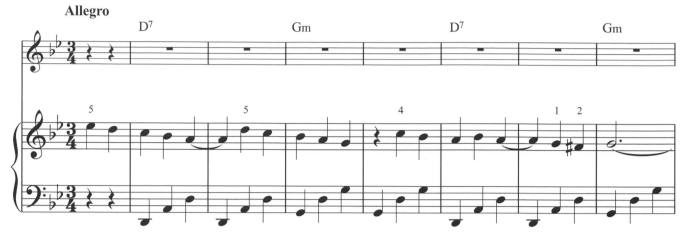

Sy. 2926

Fine

D. S. (𝄋) al Fine

Andante
from Sonata Op. 99, No. 1

James Hook (1746–1827)

Albumblatt
from *Kolibris*, Op. 210

Emil Kronke (1865–1938)

Con moto tranquillo

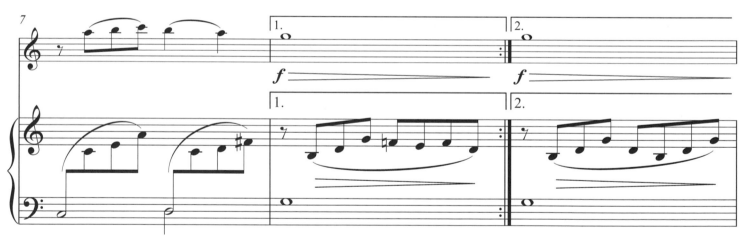

Larghetto espressivo
from Sonata Op. 25, No. 1

Johann Ludwig Dussek (1760–1812)

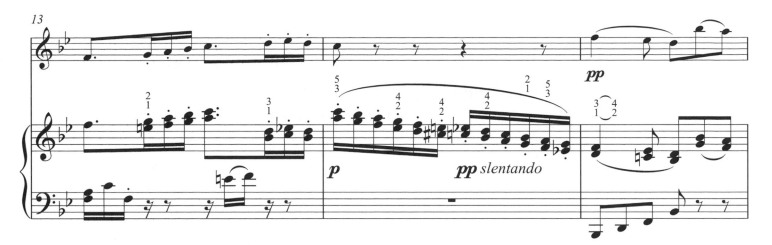

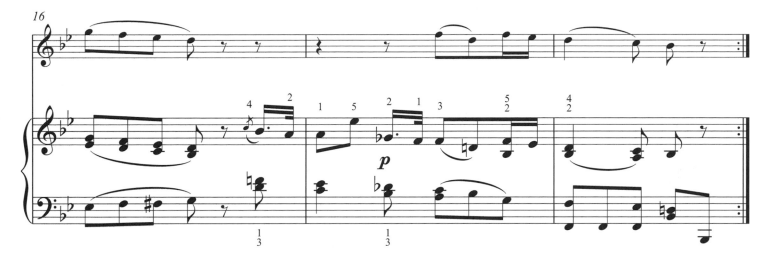

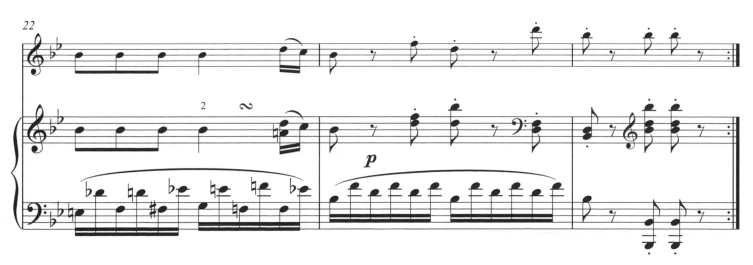

Cantabile
from Sonata in G Major, TWV 41:G8

Georg Philipp Telemann (1681–1767)
Arr.: E. Weinzierl / E. Waechter

Menuett

from Divertimento, KV 439b, No. 2

Wolfgang Amadeus Mozart (1756–1791)
Arr.: E. Weinzierl / E. Waechter

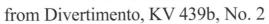

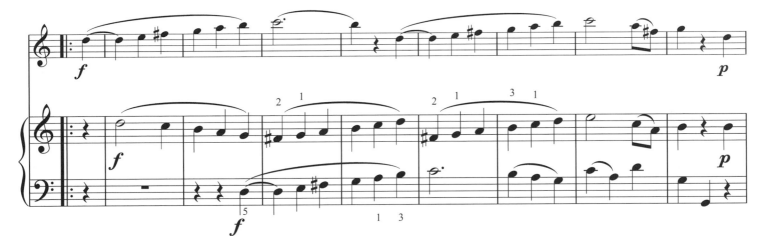

Barcarole

from the opera *Oberon*

Carl Maria von Weber (1786–1826)
Arr.: after Kaspar Kummer (1795–1870)

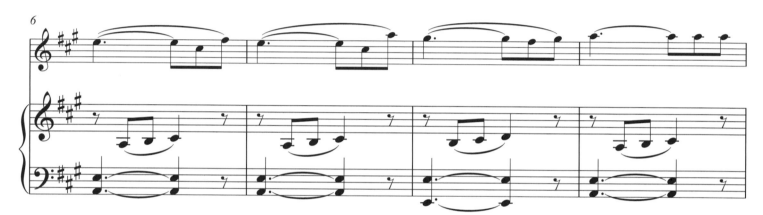

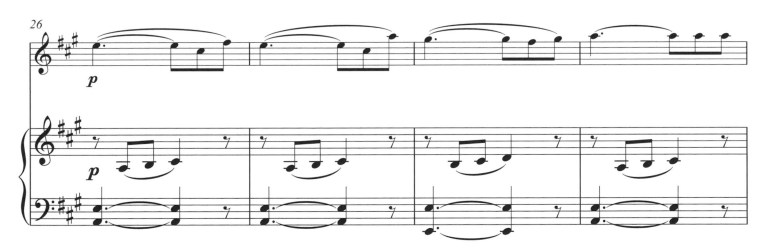

Gavotte
from the opera *Rosine*

François-Joseph Gossec (1734–1829)
Arr.: E. Weinzierl / E. Waechter
(after Ary van Leeuwen)

Sy. 2926   © 2015 by G. Ricordi & Co., Berlin

D. C. al ⊕-⊕